Justus' camera

Snap!!!

"Mooommm!!!" yells Philli,

"Justus keeps taking pictures of me".

Justus runs away laughing.

He bothers his older sister every chance he can get. He calls her his best subject because she's always busy doing fun things that he can capture with his camera.

SCHOOL

See, the children at school didn't understand why Justus took this camera everywhere.

They didn't know that he got it as a gift from his grandmother. Some of his peers gossiped that he wanted to be a professional photographer when he gets older.

Justus was really close to his grandmother before she passed away. Any time she was around, he sat on her lap and asked her to tell him stories about her childhood. Other times they would look at family photos together.

One day he exclaimed to Grandmommy, "I want to be a pictureman".

Laughing, Grandmommy asked, "What is a pictureman?"

"You know, a man who takes pictures", shrugging his shoulders.

Grandmommy replied by saying, "You can do anything you want to do".

Justus loved checking out the features of the camera on everyone's phones, but there was something about the authenticity of a polaroid.

Grandmommy gave him a polaroid camera and a few rolls of film for his 8th birthday.

You'll never see Justus without his camera. If you do, there's a guarantee that it is within arm's reach.

One morning Justus plunged out of bed. "I am up!" he yelled to Philli.

"Why are you still upstairs, you haven't eaten breakfast yet and the bus will be here in 10 minutes! What are you doing?" Philli yelled with annoyance.

Justus dove down the stairs with his backpack and jacket. He ran to the kitchen and scarfed down his bowl of cereal.

He was almost out the door when he remembered that he didn't have his camera on him.

He ran back up the stairs where his dad was already holding the camera.

"Here you go son, have a good day at school and good luck on your Picture Contest".

"Good luck Justus!" Yelled his mom.

"Good luck Justus!" Yelled Philli

"Thank you guys", Justus yelled, stumbling out the door.

On the bus he remembered the day Grandmommy handed him his gift.

HAPPY BIRTHDAY

He crossed his fingers and closed his eyes while he thanked GOD for his family and his camera.

He already knew that he had won the contest, but in a few more minutes he would know for certain when he reads his name on the bulletin board of his classroom door.

THE END

www.ingramcontent.com/pod-product-compliance
Lightning Source LLC
Chambersburg PA
CBHW040940110726
48006CB00001B/203